A FLIGHT
FIGUREHEADS

From British Warships at The Box, Plymouth

David Pulvertaft

AMBERLEY

First published 2020

Amberley Publishing
The Hill, Stroud
Gloucestershire, GL5 4EP

www.amberley-books.com

British Library Cataloguing in Publication Data.
A catalogue record for this book is available from the British Library.

ISBN 978 1 4456 9852 6 (paperback)
ISBN 978 1 4456 9853 3 (ebook)

Typeset in 10pt on 13pt Sabon.
Typesetting by Aura Technology and Software Services, India.
Printed in the UK.

Contents

Preliminary sketch for Hope. (Dickerson)

Foreword

By Admiral Sir Jonathon Band GCB, DL

It is a great pleasure for me to contribute to this book that accompanies the wonderful display of British warship figureheads at The Box in Plymouth.

As a young man newly commissioned in the Royal Navy, and as an undergraduate at Exeter University, I had time to deepen my knowledge of the Service's history. This led me to understand its relationship with the nation's development and culture and this certainly influenced my thinking during forty years of active service. I am a firm believer that successful military commanders must not only be well informed on modern strategy and technology, they must have a mature understanding of the history that has shaped their service and influenced their traditions.

It was for this reason that, when I retired from the Royal Navy in 2009, I welcomed the opportunity of becoming the Chairman of the then newly established National Museum of the Royal Navy, which had been launched that September. Formed by the amalgamation of the Royal Naval Museum (Portsmouth), the Royal Marines Museum (Eastney), the Royal Navy Submarine Museum (Gosport) and the Fleet Air Arm Museum (Yeovilton), it tells for the first time the history of all arms of the Naval Service. More recently in 2018, and as part of its regional development, the NMRN assumed responsibility for the Plymouth Naval Base Heritage Collection at Devonport. This in turn has enabled the figureheads and ships' badges from that collection to be put on permanent display to the public for the first time.

The nation's maritime history has influenced the social and cultural story of Plymouth over the years and, in this, the ships represented here have each played a small part. It is therefore very good to see their figureheads, beautifully restored and remounted to show them at their best, while David Pulvertaft's research allows the contribution of each to be better understood.

Jonathon Band

First Sea Lord 2006–2009,
Chairman, National Museum of
the Royal Navy 2009–2019

Acknowledgements

My first acknowledgements go to the four organisations that have given financial support to the publication of this book; The Box itself, the National Museum of the Royal Navy, which owns the figureheads, and the two specialist consultants: the museum designer – Event Communications – and the exhibition contractor – The Hub. Without their generosity, the project might well have been stillborn!

Three of my long-standing friends within the field of maritime history have, once again, been most helpful. Richard Blundell of Hobart, Tasmania, who inherited the Dickerson Archive from the family of Plymouth ship-carvers, has added to the drawings that I have used in the past. Richard Hunter – figurehead historian – and Lt Cdr Lawrie Phillips – author and historian – have each provided images from their extensive collections and have offered sound advice.

My thanks go to three photographers: Nick Matthews, whose expertise improved some of the images in my own collection, Dom Moore and Wayne Perry, who each captured the figureheads in the extremely trying conditions between the figureheads being painted in their new colour schemes and 'taking flight' at The Box.

I am grateful to Tim Stopford, author and publisher of *Admiralty Ships Badges*, for his permission to reproduce the original patterns where these follow the style of the figureheads on display.

I am also most grateful to the several members of staff at The Box who pulled every string that they could find to help me achieve the publisher's deadline; in particular Steve Conway whose initial responsibility was as Conservation Contracts Officer but eventually did much more!

All these people have been so helpful but any errors that remain are mine alone.

Finally, my thanks go to my wife, Mary Rose, who has been her usual supportive self despite my being distracted by this latest 'figurehead commitment'!

Introduction

Each of the figureheads that is on display at The Box was carved for an eighteenth-century warship of the Royal Navy and served on the ship's bow from the day she was launched until the completion of her service. Most of them come from the Devonport Dockyard collection and each has been specially restored and remounted for this display.

The tradition of ships being given figureheads stems from the earliest days of sail but only after an Admiralty Order of 1727 were British warships permitted to have figureheads that represented the ship's name, rather than what had been the tradition, a carved lion. From that point on, the figurehead provided a unique identity to which members of the crew could relate and some would even claim that 'the figurehead allowed the ship to see where she was going'!

The purpose of this book is to describe each of the figureheads: how and why it was carved, what places it visited and what actions it saw while on the ship's bow. Some figureheads were surprisingly mobile after they came ashore and, where this is the case, their movement is tracked. All this detail is set against the background of how figureheads developed over the years and how the carvers submitted their designs.

By illustrating the text with original figurehead drawings and designs, this book also acts as a showcase for the beautiful artwork that was created in the nineteenth-century carvers' workshops, here in Plymouth.

At the end of the book will be found a directory of all the figureheads that have, over the years, been displayed in either Devonport Dockyard or the Devonport Naval Base. From that summary, the fourteen examples that are now at The Box are put in context against those that were transferred elsewhere or were simply lost.

Development of the Figurehead

While the figureheads on display at The Box are each from a nineteenth-century warship, those from earlier centuries were given figureheads that showed that they were men of war and should therefore be treated with proper respect. The largest ships were given intricate 'group figureheads' such as the 1737 *Victory* with its crown, royal arms and Neptune riding a 'sea-horse', with matching figures of Britannia riding a 'sea-lion' on the other side.

Other English warships of the period were given a fierce lion to show that this was a fighting vessel, even though there was no indication of the name of the ship

Group Figurehead – 1737 *Victory*. (Author)   Unidentified Lion Figurehead. (Author)

in which it was serving. The lion was usually crowned, with its body curving backwards to follow the line of the ship's stem-post.

In 1727 an Admiralty Order was issued that allowed ships to be given individual figureheads that related to the ship's name, rather than the traditional lion. During the next fifty years or so, full length figures began to be carved, shaped much as the earlier lions had been with their legs following the line of the stem-post. The example illustrated here was drawn at Plymouth for *Hercule*, the French ship *L'Hercule* – captured near Brest in April 1798 and brought to Plymouth. The new figurehead was carved in 1801 before she commissioned into the Royal Navy; it shows Hercules brandishing his olive-wood club and wearing the skin of the Nemean lion that he had slain with his bare hands. In the trailboard carving may be seen the three-headed dog, Cerberus, that guarded the entrance to the underworld.

With this new freedom of design, the figurehead carvers produced a wide range of designs, the examples shown below all coming from the Dickerson workshop in Plymouth. The largest were 'standing figures' such as the beautifully drawn but unidentified warrior with a plumed helmet and rustic clothing. There are clues to the identity of the ship in the two fish-tailed children in the trailboard carving, one holding the sword and scales of justice while the other holds a badge that symbolises the City of London, but the actual ship is not identified. In the collection at The Box, standing figures are represented by the figurehead of HMS *Royal William* on page 87.

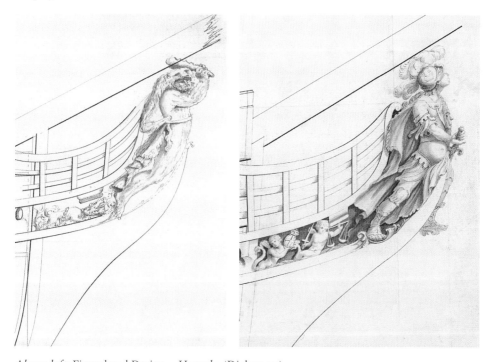

Above left: Figurehead Design – *Hercule*. (Dickerson)

Above right: Figurehead Design – Standing Figure. (Dickerson)

If the size of the ship did not justify a standing figure, a demi-head was a smaller alternative. Normally terminated at the waist, these carvings included arms and were thus able to be shown holding objects that helped to identify the ship. The design here was for the *Invincible* – a powerful name that the Dickersons portrayed by carving Zeus, the supreme ruler of the Greek gods. He was normally shown to be bearded and here wears a crown and is carrying his sceptre with an attendant eagle. More importantly, he is holding a thunderbolt, the weapon that he cast down on his enemies; another appeared as the trailboard carving. The only demi-head in the figureheads at The Box is that from HMS *Windsor Castle* – see page 81 – thus allowing Queen Victoria to be shown holding the orb and sceptre.

With the Controller of the Navy always seeking ways to save money, busts were preferred for small ships as, with their arms terminated above the elbow, they cost less to carve. However, they were no longer able to be shown holding a symbolic item and the trailboard carvings were created to provide this information. Busts are therefore well represented in the Dickerson archive, the design here being for HMS *Aboukir*, a name that celebrates Nelson's victory at the Battle of the Nile in Aboukir Bay. The bust of Admiral Nelson was approved but, as will be seen in the deletions to the trailboard carvings, these were not allowed.

By the end of the nineteenth century, ship design had developed such that figureheads were no longer appropriate, and they were discontinued. The bows of early twentieth-century ships continued to be decorated with cartouches and

Above left: Figurehead Design – HMS *Invincible*. (Dickerson)

Above right: Figurehead Design – HMS *Aboukir*. (Dickerson)

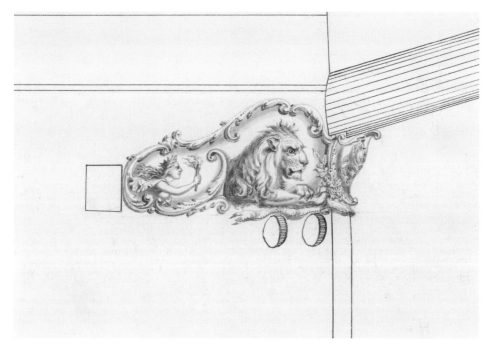

Bow Decoration Design – HMS *Zealous*. (Dickerson)

scroll-work that required the skills of the figurehead carver as will be seen from the design for HMS *Zealous*.

There remained, however, a need within the Royal Navy for ships to have an emblem of some sort and individual ship's badges began to be created, initially on an ad hoc basis but in a rationalised form from about 1919. Many of these perpetuated the identity that had been created by the figurehead tradition and, where this applies to the figureheads at The Box, the badges are reproduced in the appropriate chapter.

Colour Schemes

The question of how warship figureheads were painted when at sea has been asked by many but not satisfactorily answered until recently. Very few paint analyses had been recorded during historic figurehead restorations, probably because of lack of time or finances during these interventions and the absence of proven techniques. The fact that the vast majority of the two hundred or so surviving figureheads are painted in colour had always suggested that this was how they looked when in service; but evidence from historic paintings and photographs suggested otherwise. An article in the May 2018 *The Mariner's Mirror* concluded that both white figureheads and those painted in colour were to be seen throughout the fleet, but with rather more being painted white than in colour. It also suggested that the preponderance of coloured survivors was partly the result of the carvings sitting in dockyard buildings for over a hundred years where the temptation to smarten them up could not be resisted!

Ship Names and the Figurehead Carvers' Task

The earliest English fighting ships tended to have simple names with a warlike significance such as *Triumph*, *Revenge* and *Repulse* or compound names such as *Dreadnought*, *Swiftsure* and *Vanguard*, selected to identify the ships and inspire the sailors who lived and fought in them.

A detailed analysis of how the subject developed over the centuries may be found in Manning and Walker's seminal work, *British Warship Names*, an invaluable reference book that also lists all the individual ships and the dates that they served under that particular name.

As the figureheads that are displayed at The Box were all carved for nineteenth-century warships, a knowledge of the subjects that were then in vogue will help to understand where they fit onto the canvas of the period. As the ships were all in the Royal Navy, 'Royalty' had to be there, so we find, for example, the likeness of King William IV from the bow of HMS *Royal William* and the likeness of Queen Victoria from the bow of HMS *Windsor Castle*. There were famous people – Admiral Nelson was depicted on no less than eight ships after his death in 1805, even though none is in this collection. There were beasts and birds such as HM Ships *Centaur*, *Basilisk* and *Sphynx*. There were 'qualities' – HMS *Defiance*. There were characters from Greek and Roman mythology – HM Ships *Calliope*, *Cadmus*, *Minerva* and *Sybille*. There were geographic references – HM Ships *Calcutta* and *Tamar* – and finally there were prizes taken in battle – HMS *Topaze*. Considering the small size of the sample on display, the subjects are well represented.

In the seventeenth and eighteenth centuries, most British warship figureheads had been in the form of lions and the carvers were accomplished at carving these beasts. Most of the money that was spent on 'carved work' had its focus on the intricate work around the sterns of the ships – the overall subject being addressed in L. G. Carr Laughton's definitive book of 1925, *Old Ship Figure-Heads & Sterns*.

After the Navy Board's announcement in 1727 that, in future, carvings that represented the ship's name could be used in the place of lions, the carvers had to develop new skills. Over the subsequent decades, a wide variety of carvings were

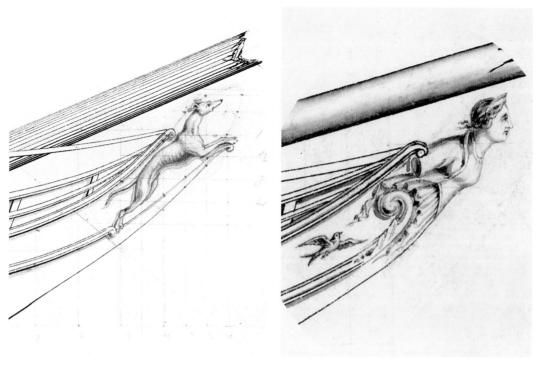

Above left: Figurehead Design – HMS *Greyhound*. (Dickerson)

Above right: Figurehead Design – HMS *Martin*. (Dickerson)

developed, and the Surveyor of the Navy took it upon his office to approve the designs and the associated costs. The changing size and structure of the fleet in Victorian times also gave rise to ships being given the names of animals. The carvers adapted to this change; large animals, such as that carved for HMS *Greyhound*, were usually given a full-length carving of the whole animal, while smaller ones, such as that carved for HMS *Martin*, might have the subject added to the trailboard. Somewhere in between, but not represented here, were examples of the animal being held in the arms of the figurehead.

The whole approval process was a lengthy and bureaucratic one but, as many of the letters and design drawings are now preserved at the National Archives, Kew, much valuable detail is available to historians.

The Figurehead Carvers of Plymouth

There were figurehead carvers at Plymouth since the late seventeenth century, eleven of them being listed in *British Figurehead and Ship Carvers* by Phil Thomas. His book includes merchant ship carvers, as well as those who carved for the Royal Navy, much of his information coming from what was then the Public Record Office, at Kew, where he had concentrated his search on the Accountant General's ledgers and the Yard Pay Books.

For the period spanned by the figureheads at The Box, it was the Dickerson family that was the most successful in winning the naval contracts. Four members of the family are described in Plymouth records as 'Carver' or 'Master Carver': Samuel, his sons James and William, and James's son, Frederick. Some of the letters from the Controller's office that give approval of the figurehead designs allow us to identify which of them carved the figurehead of a particular ship, and how their style evolved over the years.

The greatest legacy, however, that the family left to posterity, was a portfolio of original drawings that accumulated in their workshop that was eventually handed down through the family until it emerged in Hobart, Australia, in 2004. The collection of drawings was the result of the carvers' failure to follow the instructions from the office of the Controller of the Navy! Once approved by that office, the carvers were supposed to note the decision and return each design with its letter of approval. However, the Dickersons clearly needed to use the drawings as their guide to carve the actual figurehead, as is evidenced by vertical and horizontal pencil lines on some of the designs, allowing them to be 'scaled up' by a factor of 48; the designs generally being '1 inch to 4 feet'.

Samuel Dickerson worked from about 1770 and would have carved the standing figure of King George III on the bow of HMS *Royal Sovereign*, the design of which was published in the H. F. Whitfield book *Plymouth and Devonport in Times of War and Peace*. It shows the king in a frock coat and breeches, wearing a laurel wreath, and has a caption 'in the possession of Mr Sydenham'. It is known that John Lewis Sydenham was the son-in-law of Frederick Dickerson but sadly the design itself does not appear to have survived.

The earliest surviving drawing in the portfolio is the 'group' design for the 1777 *Duke*, part of which is missing from having been folded too many times. It shows the bust of King George III above the royal arms, King Neptune (holding a trident) being his supporter. From the contemporary ship plan we know that Neptune is himself supported by a cherub beside a 'sea-horse' in the trailboard carvings.

Also from Samuel Dickerson's workshop came the design in October 1798 for HMS *Castor*'s figurehead. It is unusual in that it was submitted in colour, but the subject is drawn as a warrior that he clearly felt was appropriate for one of the 'Heavenly Twins', sons of Zeus.

In 1790 Samuel had been joined by his son, James Dickerson, who, by 1794, was describing himself as a 'Master Carver' and was advertising for a 'ship carver's apprentice'. A man of some standing, he had his portrait painted as a young man.

Figurehead Design –
HMS *Castor*.
(Dickerson)

James Dickerson, Master Carver. (Dickerson)

It was not only the largest warships that received the attention of the Devonport carvers. When James Dickerson submitted his design for HMS *Plymouth* in 1796, it was said to be an 'Admiralty Yacht, 8 eight guns' but was actually built for the use of senior dockyard officers. The figurehead was described in the letter forwarding the design as 'Ceres holding a cornucopia in one hand and a wreath of corn in the other, standing erect on the knee clothed in rich drapery'. No expense was spared for decorating this statement of local prestige, the carver having been paid the very handsome sum of £96.7.6 for the carved work, of which £11 was for the figurehead.

By 1806, James was also producing designs that met the controller's drive for simpler and less expensive busts. Two ships that had fought at the Battle of Trafalgar – HMS *Conqueror* and HMS *Achille* – returned to Plymouth for repairs, including the provision of new figureheads. Rather than designs being submitted to the Controller of the Navy, a visit by Admiralty officials to the dockyard was used to obtain approval and two fine busts were carved. As they were approved locally, the designs do not feature in the documents at the National Archives but were amongst those in the Dickerson portfolio.

Figurehead Design – HMS *Plymouth*. (Dickerson)

The captain of HMS *Conqueror* requested that, rather than the new figurehead being carved in the likeness of William the Conqueror, it should be a bust of the hero of Trafalgar, Lord Nelson. The normal convention for ship plans – from which the ship was built – was to have the bow to the right and the stern to the left. To conform with this, figurehead designs were normally shown facing the right but, as will be seen overleaf, the bust of Nelson faces left so that the distinctive 'chelenk' that the admiral wore in his hat could be seen. Once complete, Captain Pellew and his officers paid for the figurehead to be gilded, the local newspaper reporting:

When the ship went down the harbour, and as the sun shone on the head of the Conqueror, it cut a most brilliant appearance to the spectators on the Hoe.

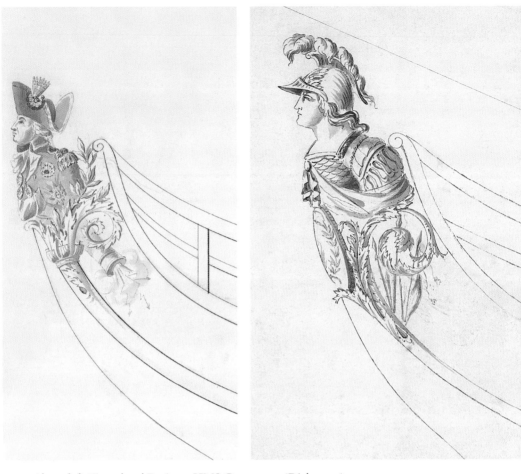

Above left: Figurehead Design – HMS *Conqueror*. (Dickerson)

Above right: Figurehead Design – HMS *Achille*. (Dickerson)

HMS *Achille* used the French spelling of Achilles, as was the custom when her predecessor had been a French prize. Achilles is shown in armour, as would be expected for one of the great heroes of Green mythology, facing to the left probably to match his companion in the portfolio, Lord Nelson.

Finally, Frederick Dickerson joined the family business in 1832 just as the figurehead for HMS *Royal William* was being carved. The design is not to be found at the National Archives, but a hastening letter shows that it was certainly carved at Plymouth. Its story and that of its replacement will be found on pages 86 to 91.

Frederick was the most successful of the Dickersons, carving many figureheads for ships building at Plymouth and Pembroke Dock. Some of his designs were traditional – such as that for the 1840 HMS *London*, wearing a 'mural crown' to signify a city and with the symbols of the City of London in the trailboards. Other designs showed more imagination, such as that for the 1849 HMS *Megaera* – one of the 'Furies' of Greek mythology with snakes instead of hair.

Above left: Figurehead Design – HMS *London*. (Dickerson)

Above right: Figurehead Design – HMS *Megaera*. (Dickerson)

When Frederick Dickerson retired, he took with him a portfolio of over 140 drawings of all shapes and sizes, including preliminary sketches and heraldic devices, but mostly detailed designs for individual ships. They passed through descendants of the Dickersons until they eventually arrived in Hobart, Tasmania. In 2004, the owner, Richard Blundell, told the Royal Naval Museum of his inheritance and, since then, has been most generous in allowing the present author to use the material in talks, articles and books. The collection was recently sold to the National Maritime Museum, Greenwich, where it will be catalogued and become accessible to the public online.

The Devonport Figurehead Collection

When warships came to the end of their useful life, some were sold to commercial shipbreakers to be broken up while others were taken to pieces in the Royal Dockyards, allowing fittings and sound timbers to be reused. Figureheads presented a particular problem as, having taken on the mantle of the 'spirit' of the ship, it would have been hardly right to burn them on a bonfire! Thus, figureheads accumulated in the Royal Dockyards at Chatham, Plymouth and Portsmouth, being laid aside in large spaces such as sail-lofts and rigging houses and eventually forming the basis of dockyard museums.

At Plymouth, a building that had originally been the shipwrights' work shed was appropriated by the Admiral Superintendent of the yard as 'a repository of the

Fire at H M Dockyard Plymouth, 1840. (The Box)

trophies of earlier wars' and named Adelaide Row in honour of the then Queen Dowager – the widow of King William IV.

That collection came to a dramatic end when, on the night of 27 September 1840, a fire broke out in HMS *Talavera*, refitting in one of the docks. It spread through Adelaide Row and consumed HMS *Imogene* in the adjacent dock. Heroic efforts by fire-fighters prevented the fire spreading further but both ships and the historic collection were destroyed.

The contemporary account of the fire lists many of the relics that were destroyed, allowing the sixteen figureheads whose details were given to be included in the Plymouth figurehead directory at the end of this book.

As more ships were taken to pieces at Devonport, the figurehead collection began to grow again such that, by the end of the nineteenth century, articles appeared in magazines such as *The Strand Magazine* and *Leisure Hour*, initially with line drawings of the carvings and then with photographs. Then in 1911 the Admiralty published the *Admiralty Catalogue of Pictures, Plate, Relics &c.* that listed its holdings, including figureheads. Although these were only a minor part of the catalogue, each was identified with the particular ship for which it had been carved, its size and a brief description – a most useful baseline against which all subsequent groupings can be assessed. The figureheads were listed geographically, the dockyard collections being dominant but with small clusters elsewhere such as that at the boys' training establishment in Suffolk, HMS *Ganges*. The list of those at Devonport Dockyard was the longest, containing no less than sixty-five figureheads.

Spurred on, no doubt, by the Admiralty Catalogue, the Society for Nautical Research published two articles in its journal, *The Mariner's Mirror*, in which the

The Fire Engine House, Devonport – *c.* 1897. (Hunter)

Hon. Secretary wrote of visits that he had made to the dockyards in 1913. Using the Admiralty Catalogue as his guide, he described how the Devonport collection was housed in three buildings: the Fire Engine House, the Rigging House and the Police Parade Shed, with the largest carvings standing guard in prominent places outside. He was clearly impressed with what he had seen but concluded that 'such splendid national relics should be in a great Naval Museum; but this, to our shame, we still lack'. He also asked, 'Is there no one who will take this matter in hand?'

As the twentieth century saw fewer warships with figureheads being taken to pieces, the Devonport collection remained largely unchanged until 1936 when the National Maritime Museum was created at Greenwich. Part of the Admiralty's contribution to its core collection was the gift of twenty figureheads from Devonport. More changes were to come as bombing during the Second World War devastated much of Plymouth and Devonport Dockyard was the major industrial target. Ten figurehead losses from that time are identified in the figurehead directory at the end of the book, one of them being the fine standing figure from HMS *St George* that stood just inside the dockyard gate.

The second half of the twentieth century saw further losses but, rather than by enemy action, these examples were lost by a failure to understand the effects of decay. In both Chatham and Devonport, it was believed that a coat of resin and/or fibreglass

HMS *St George* – 1936. (Author)

would protect the wood and that the figureheads could still be safely displayed out of doors. Sadly, this was not a long-term solution and many of the figureheads that were so treated and then transferred to Naval establishments to encourage a sense of history and tradition were lost. Once more the figurehead directory will provide some detail.

As the twentieth century came to a close and the losses over the decades became apparent, the figureheads at Devonport were gradually brought under cover to dry out and many were displayed once again in the Fire Engine House, by then part of the Plymouth Naval Base Visitor Centre.

The creation of the National Museum of the Royal Navy in 2009 stimulated new interest in the collection and in 2012 Hugh Harrison – Consultant and Contractor in the Conservation of Joinery and Polychromed Timber – wrote his first report for the museum describing the condition of each figurehead, the extent of fibreglass and resin that had been applied to them in the 1950s and how the moisture content of the timber varied. It also gave general guidance on how further deterioration should be avoided in the short term.

In a second report, this time written in 2016 for the Plymouth City Council, he was joined by specialists in non-destructive testing and architectural paint conservation. The non-destructive testing part of the report included moisture measurements and the results of micro-drillings to test the condition of the underlying wood. The results varied enormously. The paint conservation part of the report gave a good feel for how multi-layered paint surfaces and resin could be removed, again varying from figurehead to figurehead. What that second report also provided for the first time was an estimate of the cost of conserving, repainting and rehanging those figureheads that might be selected for the unique opportunity offered by Mayflower 400, planned for the Spring of 2020.

By the end of 2017, the selection of which figureheads should be included at The Box was agreed, based on the historical significance of each carving, its condition and the estimated cost of conservation. Two figureheads were selected for a pilot intervention – from HMS *Topaze* and HMS *Royal William* – to establish a 'conservation treatment plan' and what new mounting arrangements would be necessary.

The scene was set for conservation to begin and structural engineers to design how the heavy and delicate relics of the 'Sailing Navy' could be safely displayed.

Figureheads at The Box

Twelve of the fourteen figureheads that are on display at The Box came from the bow of a British warship, having previously been part of the Devonport Collection. The exceptions are that named *Minerva*, which was probably never fitted to a ship, and that from HMS *Calcutta*, which was only acquired by the National Museum of the Royal Navy in 2011 when it needed urgent attention. The chapters that follow provide details of those that were assessed as being in suitable condition for conservation and long-term display and, happily, include a variety of differing service histories.

During 2017 the selected figureheads were despatched for the conservation work to start. Orbis Conservation of Greenwich received the figureheads from HM Ships *Sybille*, *Topaze*, *Calcutta*, *Tamar* and *Royal William*; Hugh Harrison of West Anstey, Devon, received those from HM Ships *Defiance* and *Windsor Castle*; and Mainmast Conservation of Little Trethvas, Cornwall, received those from HM Ships *Calliope*, *Sphynx*, *Basilisk*, *Centaur*, *Cadmus*, *Aurora* and the standing figure of Minerva.

This book is not the place to record the details of what conservation techniques were necessary for individual figureheads, but the following played an invaluable part. 3D laser scanning allowed the exterior form of each carving to be recorded for remodelling and to help the structural engineers calculate the centres of gravity for new mounting arrangements. Sonic tomography, normally used to assess the health of living trees, was used to identify areas of decay for treatment and consolidation to avoid further deterioration. The resin skins were painstakingly removed or – in some instances – used as a mould to replace missing pieces before the new colour scheme was applied.

Suffice to say, the management at The Box, in conjunction with the three conservation specialists, developed a range of conservation methodologies that allowed the figureheads to be saved, the beauty of their original carving to be better seen and each one made strong enough to be put on display. It is a piece of good fortune that the decision was taken when it was to conserve the figureheads for display, otherwise some would, undoubtedly, have been lost for ever. As for the future, the techniques that have been developed for this collection will be invaluable for future conservation projects as there are still many British warship figureheads that would benefit from such treatment.

Colour Schemes

As was reported on page 11 under the 'Development of the Figurehead', some warship figureheads were painted in colour when serving at sea, while rather more were painted white. As the conservation of this group involved stripping the paint and resin/fibreglass coatings, there were opportunities to analyse how they had been painted in the past, even though the evidence depended on how effective previous restorers had been in stripping historic layers of paint. Not surprisingly, most of the examinations were inconclusive but two were shown by microscopic examinations

HMS *Sybille* – 1912. (Player's Cigarettes)   HMS *Calcutta* – 1912. (Player's Cigarettes)

of paint layers to have been painted white when in service, namely HM Ships *Windsor Castle* and *Royal William.*

For the display at The Box, it was decided that a mixture of white and coloured figureheads would not show the group as a whole to its best, and yet the modern paints that had been applied in previous restorations made them appear too brash. Inspiration came from a set of twenty-five cigarette cards published by John Player & Sons in 1912. While this may appear an unusual source of information upon which to base decisions on a paint scheme, the cigarette card artist, in 1912, must have had access to the figureheads to paint their portraits and had chosen a soft colour palette for his paintings. It was decided that a similar palette should be used at The Box. Of the twenty-five cigarette cards in the set, two happen to be amongst those now on display, those from HM Ships *Sybille* and *Calcutta.*

Battle Honours, Ships Badges, Etc.

In the chapters that follow, there are several themes that thread their way through the descriptions of the individual ships. Battle honours are awarded to ships of the Royal Navy for 'successful war service' and are then displayed on an honours board by all successive ships of the same name. The earliest battle so recorded was Armada 1588 and they continue to be awarded to this day. Those that are included in the ship chapters that follow were awarded to the ship during the figurehead's period of service, and therefore provide an operational bond between individual ships in the display.

Ships badges are also a feature of today's Royal Navy, continuing an artistic representation of the ships' names that had previously been achieved by their figureheads. The wall display of badges celebrates this art form and, for those ships where there is a connection between the figurehead and the more modern ships badge, the badge is included in the relevant chapter of this book – see HM Ships *Sphynx, Basilisk* and *Centaur.* By chance, these three badges are of different shapes; the offset square being allocated to sloops, the shield to destroyers and the circular frame to capital ships. From 1940 these were rationalised, and all warships today have badges of the circular form.

The final thread that links the individual figureheads has its origin in a renewed interest in maritime history in the 1930s. Photographs were taken for an annotated album of the 'Figureheads in Naval Establishments in the Plymouth Command'. As this created a snapshot of the Devonport collection shortly before the Second World War, the relevant photographs of those in today's display have been included to give an idea of what has changed over the last eighty years.

Preliminary sketch for Hercules. (Dickerson)

HMS *Calliope*

Built in Sheerness Dockyard and launched there in October 1837, HMS *Calliope* was a Sixth Rate ship of twenty-eight guns. Her figurehead was a female three-quarter-length bust wearing an eastern crown.

As there was no resident carver at Sheerness at that time, the Dockyard Superintendent asked for a figurehead to be provided and the Controller of the Navy invited Robert Hall, of Rotherhithe, and J. E. Hellyer, of Portsmouth, to submit designs and estimates. The carvers of the day were well informed about Greek mythology and, as Calliope had been the Muse of Epic Poetry, submitted appropriate designs.

Robert Hall forwarded sketches of three different demi-figures in a pastoral style: one holding a lute, one holding a trumpet and one holding a paper and quill-pen. Each was estimated as costing £7.0.0.

The Hellyers submitted two designs: the demi-figure – shown here at £7.10.0 – and a bust with the document and wreath in the trailboards at £6.0.0. As the Controller of the Navy was always looking for good value for money, the Hellyer bust was approved.

Between 1838 and 1839 HMS *Calliope* served on the South American Station and then in the Pacific on operations up the Canton and Yangtze rivers during the First Anglo-Chinese War. She was awarded the battle honour 'China 1841–2'. An incident when up the Canton River involved her figurehead and was described by one of her crew. The ship had been towed upriver by a 'steamer', but she ran aground for twenty-four hours and had to lighten herself by unloading her anchors and shot into a junk. Once afloat again, they retired downstream 'much to the disappointment of the 'Calliope' for she had been wounded in many places in her body and breast'.

HMS *Calliope* returned home to Plymouth in March 1843 and, after minor work, recommissioned in 1845 and was despatched to the East Indies Station as part of a force to quell rebellion in New Zealand. She was awarded the battle honour 'New Zealand 1846–7'. Returning to Plymouth again in 1849 for further

Hellyer Design – HMS *Calliope*.
(The National Archives)

repairs, she recommissioned in 1850 for service on the Australian Station, where she remained until 1855. She finally paid off in Plymouth, first as a floating chapel and then as a factory ship. She was taken to pieces in Devonport Dockyard in 1883.

Her figurehead was preserved in the dockyard, initially in the Rigging House, where, in 1913, it was recorded that beneath her necklace was suspended 'a chain-shot with staple (? 3 lb shot), said to have been dug out of the lady's breast'. Perhaps this was the very shot that had wounded her when on the Canton River seventy-two years earlier!

By 1936 the records show that she was displayed in front of the victualling office of the RN barracks but, happily, she was then brought into the drill-shed of HMS *Drake* and has been indoors ever since.

The restoration and remounting of the figurehead in preparation for the display at The Box was undertaken by Mainmast Conservation of Little Trethvas, near Helston, Cornwall. The fibreglass coating that had been applied during the 1950s–60s was carefully removed to reveal the quality of her original carving.

HMS *Calliope* – 1936. (Author)

HMS *Sphynx*

Built in Woolwich Dockyard and launched there in February 1846, HMS *Sphynx* was a wooden paddle sloop of the Driver class. Her figurehead was a bust of a bearded male wearing a turban and a tunic with decorated lapels and waistband.

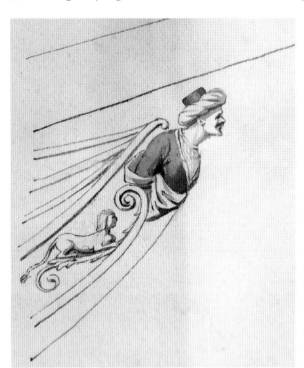

Hellyer Design - HMS *Sphynx*.
(The National Archives)

As Woolwich Dockyard did not have a resident figurehead carver at the time, the Admiral Superintendent asked the Surveyor of the Navy for a figurehead to be supplied and Hellyer & Son of Portsmouth were instructed to submit a design for approval. Two designs were offered: a sphynx at £8.10.0 or a bust head with a sphynx on each side at £9.0.0. The latter was approved. The design is typical for a small ship of the period; a bust that was intended to look like an Egyptian, with carvings of a sphinx in the trailboards that would distinguish the ship from others with figureheads of a similar form. It should be noted that, while later ships of the same name were spelt in the more usual 'Sphinx', the 1846 ship and one other were spelt 'Sphynx'.

Like many other paddle sloops of the period, HMS *Sphynx* was deployed widely during her service. In 1850 she was sent to the East Indies Station, during the Second Anglo-Burmese War, after Burma had failed to honour the 1826 treaty that followed the First Burma War. HMS *Sphynx* was awarded the battle honour 'Burma 1852–53'. After returning home she recommissioned in 1854, first for the Baltic – battle honour 'Baltic 1854' – and then for the Mediterranean and Black Sea, taking part in the bombardment of Sebastopol – battle honour 'Crimea 1854–55'. She recommissioned, again, in 1859 for the East Indies and China, being awarded the battle honour 'China 1860'. In 1862 she landed her Naval Brigade 10 miles south of Shanghai during the Taiping rebellion. One of her sailors, Able Seaman George Hinckley, rescued two of his companions under heavy fire and was awarded the Victoria Cross. HMS *Sphynx* subsequently saw service on the North America and West Indies Station before returning to Plymouth.

With such varied deployments, the turbaned Egyptian on the bow of HMS *Sphynx* (now at The Box) would have sailed in the Baltic with the standing figure of King William IV on the bow of HMS *Royal William* and would have seen action on the China Station with the mythological half-man, half-horse on the bow of HMS *Centaur*!

HMS *Sphynx* was taken to pieces in Devonport Dockyard in 1881 and her figurehead was added to that collection, being listed there in the 1911 Admiralty Catalogue. The more detailed descriptive list of the Devonport Collection, published in 1913, does not include him but, in all probability, he was amongst the smaller figureheads then housed in the Police Parade Shed.

By 1936 he was to be found in a garden beside the south office block of the RN barracks, but by 1961 he had been moved to the entrance to HMS *Cambridge*, the gunnery range at Wembury. When that establishment closed in 2001, he was transferred to the Plymouth Naval Base Museum in the Devonport's South Yard.

For the present exhibition he was restored and remounted by Mainmast Conservation of Little Trethvas near Helston, Cornwall.

The image of a sphinx lived on after our ship was taken to pieces in 1881, as her 1882 successor had a sphinx as her figurehead, while the 1939 minesweeper had a ships badge that incorporated a sphinx couchant.

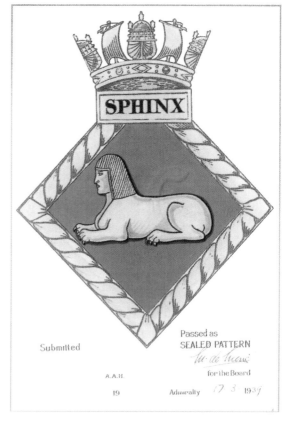

HMS *Sphynx* – 1936. (Author)   Ships Badge – HMS *Sphynx*. (Stopford)

HMS *Basilisk*

Built in Woolwich Dockyard and launched there in August 1848, HMS *Basilisk* was a wooden paddle sloop. Her figurehead was a female bust wearing an eastern crown.

As Woolwich Dockyard did not have a resident figurehead carver at the time, the Dockyard Superintendent asked the Surveyor of the Navy for a figurehead to be supplied, and Hellyer & Son of Rotherhithe were instructed to submit a design for approval. While the records at the National Archives show that the design was approved, the design drawing itself is not amongst the papers and one can only imagine the difficulty the carvers had in representing a basilisk – a legendary creature, being a snake with the wings of a cockerel and a dragon's tail that could kill by simply looking at its prey! While the surviving figurehead is a bust of a female warrior wearing what in heraldic terms was called an 'eastern crown', it would, in all probability, have been accompanied by trailboard carvings of the carver's interpretation of a basilisk.

With the benefits of steam propulsion becoming evident to the Royal Navy, several trials were conducted to establish whether paddle wheels or propellers were the more efficient means of propulsion. The first trial was a 'tug-of-war' between HMS *Alecto* and HMS *Rattler* in 1845 but was repeated in 1849 between HMS *Basilisk* and HMS *Niger*. In each case, screw propulsion was proved to be the more efficient, thus influencing the propulsion arrangements for future ships of the Royal Navy.

HMS *Basilisk*'s first active service was in the Baltic in 1854. France and Britain had become alarmed at Russia's expansion in the Black Sea and, having declared war, sent a combined fleet to the Baltic to contain the Russians. It was the first occasion on which a fleet that was made up largely of steam-driven ships was deployed; all part of the transition from sail to steam. Numerous ships of the line were involved but HMS *Basilisk* – being only a paddle sloop – played her part too and was awarded the battle honour 'Baltic 1854–55'.

She served in the West Indies between 1856 and 1860 and on the China Station between 1865 and 1869, but it was the surveying work in Australian waters for which she is best remembered. From 1872 she surveyed much of the south and east coasts of New Guinea, raising the British flag to claim the area for Britain and naming Port Moresby in honour of the commanding officer's father, Admiral Sir Fairfax Moresby. She was also tasked with putting down the practice of 'blackbirding' in Australian waters – the recruiting by force or deception of native labour to work in the sugarcane plantations of Queensland.

She eventually returned to Britain and in 1882 was taken to pieces in Chatham Dockyard. Her figurehead was added to the Chatham collection, being listed there in the 1911 Admiralty Catalogue. By the late 1950s, when the disposal of the Chatham collection was being discussed, the *Basilisk* figurehead was on display at the Gun Wharf of Chatham and was allocated to the Flag Officer Sea Training, then based at Portland. When the training task moved to Devonport in 1995, the *Basilisk* figurehead was also moved and was sited outside the new FOST headquarters. Years of standing outside in all weathers had, however, taken their toll and late in 2000 she fell off her pedestal. She was restored by Devonport Management Ltd and thereafter was displayed indoors in the Plymouth Naval Base Museum.

Above left: HMS *Basilisk* – 1990 at Portland. (Author)

Above right: Ships Badge – HMS *Basilisk*. (Stopford)

The restoration and remounting of the figurehead in preparation for the display at The Box was undertaken by Mainmast Conservation of Little Trethvas, near Helston, Cornwall.

When, in 1929, the destroyer HMS *Basilisk* was built, a ships badge was created for her, including a standing basilisk. In all probability a carving such as this would have been included on the figurehead's trailboards.

HMS *Centaur*

Built in Portsmouth Dockyard and launched there in October 1845, HMS *Centaur* was a wooden paddle frigate. Her figurehead was in the form of a full-length male centaur.

Figurehead Design –
HMS *Centaur*. (Dickerson)

   This 1845 paddle frigate was the fourth ship in the Royal Navy to be named after the race of Greek mythological creatures that had the body and legs of a horse and the torso, head and arms of a man. The previous ship of the name – a Third Rate of 1797 – had also been given a full-length centaur as her figurehead, designed by the Dickersons of Plymouth.

   Although the Hellyers of Portsmouth had submitted a design for the 1845 ship, it was not approved, and they were instructed to carve one to a design that had been supplied by the Surveyor of the Navy. It was a more delicate carving than that created for the earlier ship and thus more suitable for the smaller paddle frigate. Having been launched in Portsmouth, she was moved to East India Dock for her machinery to be fitted and was not completed in Portsmouth until February 1849.

   It is surprising how widely these small ships of the Royal Navy travelled. In the case of HMS *Centaur*, she started her operational life off the west coast of Africa, capturing two slaver ships in 1849 and two more in 1850. After recommissioning in Portsmouth, she served off the east coast of South America in 1853–54 and then in the Baltic in 1854, being awarded the battle honour 'Baltic 1855'. Recommissioning again in 1859, she joined the East Indies and China Station, being awarded the battle honour 'China 1860'. She stayed in the Far East until 1863 when she returned to Devonport where she was taken to pieces in the dockyard.

Of the figureheads suspended in The Box, the mythological figure from the bow of HMS *Centaur* would have patrolled the waters of the Baltic with the Indian figure on the bow of HMS *Calcutta* and would have seen action on the China Station with the turbaned Egyptian figure on the bow of HMS *Sphynx*!

Her figurehead was added to the Devonport figurehead collection, being listed there in the 1911 Admiralty Catalogue. Over the years he was to be found in the RN Barracks, beside the cricket pitch in HMS *Drake*, in the drill shed and eventually in the Plymouth Naval Base Museum. The restoration and remounting of the figurehead, in preparation for the display at The Box, was undertaken by Mainmast Conservation of Little Trethvas, near Helston, Cornwall.

The image of a centaur continued into the Royal Navy's post-figurehead period in the ships badge of the 1947 aircraft carrier HMS *Centaur*.

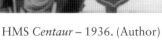

HMS *Centaur* – 1936. (Author)   Ships Badge – HMS *Centaur*. (Stopford)

HMS *Cadmus*

Built in Chatham Dockyard and launched there in May 1856, HMS *Cadmus* was a wooden screw corvette. Her figurehead was of a male bust wearing an eastern crown.

As Chatham Dockyard did not have a resident figurehead carver at the time, the Dockyard Superintendent asked the Surveyor of the Navy for a figurehead to be supplied and Messrs Hellyer & Co., of Blackwall, were instructed to submit a design for approval. The design and estimate for £10 were subsequently approved.

While the design drawings are not filed at the National Archives with the letters of approval, the Hellyers will have known that, in Greek mythology, Cadmus was the son of the king of Tyre and so was carved as a bearded male wearing an 'eastern crown' and a square-necked tunic of scale armour.

HMS *Cadmus* saw service, first on the North America and West Indies Station for ten years and then in home waters as part of the Flying Squadron. In 1869 she became the subject of local interest when, on passage from Portland to Devonport and in thick fog, she was holed by rocks at the entrance to Salcombe harbour in South Devon. Unable to stem the leak while afloat, she was run onto the Salcombe Bar until divers and shipwrights arrived to make repairs to enable her to be towed to Devonport.

In 1871 she joined the Detached Squadron and saw service in China before paying off in 1874. The ship was taken to pieces in Devonport Dockyard in 1879 and her figurehead was mounted at the south-west corner of the parade ground of the RN Barracks. While an early photograph of the ship shows that her figurehead was then painted white with a gilt crown, by the time he was displayed ashore, he had been painted in colour.

HMS *Cadmus* – Ashore on Salcombe Bar. (Illustrated London News)

In 1954 the figurehead was transferred to the garden of Admiralty House, Mount Wise, and it was probably at this time that he was coated with resin and fibreglass in the hope that this would protect him while on display out of doors.

When stripped in preparation for the display at The Box, he was found to be in particularly poor condition and every effort had to be made to save him becoming a total loss. This was one of the examples of decay that had been caught just in time. The work was undertaken by Mainmast Conservation of Little Trethvas, near Helston, Cornwall.

HMS *Cadmus* – 1936.
(Author)

A Figure of Minerva

Although this figurehead has been attributed for many years to the 1822 HMS *Minerva*, it is not believed that she was ever installed on that ship. The carving is a standing figure of Minerva holding a lance in her right hand with her left hand resting on her shield.

This carving stood for over a century beside the pathway leading up to the King's Hill Gazebo, in what later became known as Devonport's 'South Yard'. The gazebo was built in 1822 at the southernmost end of the dockyard in memory of King George III, who had once visited the site. In front of the figurehead was a shield inscribed 'MINERVA Built 1820'. While that would appear to provide watertight provenance for the carving, the history of the ship tells a different story.

HMS *Minerva* was indeed launched at Portsmouth in June 1820, a Fifth Rate ship of forty-six guns. Records at the National Archives, Kew, include the figurehead design for the ship submitted by Edward Hellyer & Son in March 1819 with an estimate of £15. It shows a standing figure with a shield – very similar to the surviving carving – but the design was not approved, the Surveyor of the Navy requiring a cheaper bust of Minerva to be carved.

The 1820 HMS *Minerva* never commissioned and, after years in Ordinary – with her masts and rigging removed – she became a floating workshop at Portsmouth and was eventually sold in 1895 to the Bevis Engineering and Shipbreaking Co.

Minerva – 1936. (Author)

for breaking up. Her figurehead did, however, survive and, as had been directed by the Surveyor in 1820, it was a simple bust of Minerva. The bust was kept by the Bevis family for many years until, in 1967, it was offered to the Victory Museum, Portsmouth, for restoration. It is still on display in the figurehead gallery of the National Museum of the Royal Navy at Portsmouth.

The most likely explanation for the standing figure at Devonport is that, having been carved by the Hellyers in anticipation of their design being approved, it became redundant and it was decided that it would make an attractive addition to the newly created King's Hill Gazebo. The figure is certainly intended to represent Minerva as the shield by her side has the severed head of Medusa carved upon it and was listed as such in the 1911 *Admiralty Catalogue of Pictures, Plate, Relics, &c.*, even though the words on the plaque were incorrect.

In the 1936 photograph, the shield is partially obscured by a free-standing cockerel – another symbol of Minerva – that had also been included in the Hellyer design of 1819. The carving had been restored on several occasions over the years and, with the chance of it being safely preserved indoors, a replica was made in 2019 for reinstatement at the gazebo, allowing the original to be displayed at The Box. Creation of the replica and repainting the original was undertaken by Mainmast Conservation of Little Trethvas, near Helston, Cornwall.

HMS *Sybille*

Built in Pembroke Dockyard and launched there in April 1847, HMS *Sybille* was a thirty-six-gun frigate. Her figurehead was a three-quarter-length female bust.

The first British warship to be named after the character from classical mythology who had the gift of prophecy was the *Sibyl*, built in 1779. When the French ship *La Sibylle* was captured in the Mediterranean in 1794 and brought into Royal Naval service, she was given the French-sounding name but spelt *Sybille*. The 1847 ship continued that arrangement as did later ships of that name until after the First World War.

As Pembroke Dockyard did not employ a resident figurehead carver, the Controller of the Navy invited the Admiral Superintendent at Devonport to provide a figurehead design and estimate for approval. Frederick Dickerson submitted a design in June 1844 with an estimated cost of £10. The design was unusual in that it was submitted in colour, probably to impress the Controller of the Navy as competition for such work was fierce. Drawn as a female bust, the design and estimate were approved.

A year later, when the figurehead was being prepared for installation, it was assessed as being 'badly carved and out of proportion'. The Controller demanded

Hellyer Design – HMS *Sybille*. (The National Archives)

to know who had examined and approved the work prior to the bill being paid and declared the figurehead 'unfit for service'! He then instructed the Admiral Superintendent at Portsmouth to arrange for the Hellyers to submit a figurehead design, which they did in August 1845 with a cost estimate of £18.

As the Hellyers will have known that Sibyl was the name of a mythical female who had been given the gift of prophecy by Apollo, they drew her wearing a classical dress with a veil flowing from her hair and a book and wand in the trailboards, alluding, no doubt, to the prophecies that she uttered on behalf of the gods. This traditional three-quarter-length female bust was approved, as was the estimate of £18.

Even though it was forty years since the death of Lord Nelson, interest in his relationship with Lady Hamilton was still active. One suggestion in an illustrated magazine of the day was that the figurehead was carved in the likeness of Lady Hamilton, whose portrait had been painted in the costume of a sibyl. If this was the case, the Hellyers seem to have failed to make that connection as it is not the most flattering design!

HMS *Sybille* eventually commissioned in 1853 and sailed for the East Indies and China Station, where she took part in the Second China War, including the bombardment of Canton, in 1856, and the Battle of Fatshan Creek, in 1857. She was awarded the battle honour 'China 1856–60'. How interesting that this classical figure and the Indian ruler on the bow of HMS *Calcutta* – both now suspended at The Box – might well have come face to face in Chinese waters over 160 years ago.

HMS *Sybille* returned to Plymouth in 1858 and was eventually sold to Marshall of Plymouth in 1866 for breaking up. Her figurehead was, however, taken into the Devonport collection, an early photograph of her being included in an 1897 issue of *The Navy and Army Illustrated*, standing on a plinth close to the dockyard church.

The figurehead was listed in the 1911 *Admiralty Catalogue of Pictures, Plate, Relics &c.* and was also included in the set of twenty-five cigarette cards issued, in 1912, by John Player & Sons, as already seen in the introduction to the figurehead chapters.

By 1913, the figurehead was included in the article on the Devonport collection, published in *The Mariner's Mirror* by the Hon. Secretary of the Society for Nautical Research, as being in the vicinity of the South Entrance to the dockyard, but he was not impressed with the quality of the work, describing her as being 'rather poor and simpering'. In 1936, when the collection was photographed for the Plymouth Command album, she was still there but she had not completed her travels.

In 1947, HMS *Sea Eagle*, the Joint Anti-Submarine School at Londonderry, requested that a figurehead should be provided to represent the naval part of their role and Sybille was transferred. She remained there when the base was handed over to the Army in 1971, becoming Ebrington Barracks, but when the Army moved out, the figurehead returned to Devonport to rejoin the collection that she had left more than fifty years earlier.

The restoration and re-mounting of the figurehead, in preparation for the display at The Box, was undertaken by Orbis Conservation of Greenwich. Did their work

HMS *Sybille* –
1936. (Author)

explain how an 1846 design of a three-quarter-length bust, following the curve of the ship's bow, was transformed into a standing figure by 1897, when she was first photographed ashore? While no exploratory work was undertaken by Orbis Conservation, by the time her paint had been stripped and an undercoat applied, joints in her structure could be seen that suggest that additional timber had been added, and the folds of her dress had been extended to show her as she is today. Useful work, no doubt, for the craftsmen of the dockyard.

Preliminary sketch for Justice. (Dickerson)

HMS *Aurora*

Built in Pembroke Dockyard and launched there in June 1861, HMS *Aurora* was a wooden screw frigate of forty-one guns. Her figurehead was a three-quarter-length female bust representing the Roman Goddess of the Dawn.

As Pembroke Dockyard did not employ a resident figurehead carver, the Surveyor of the Navy invited the Superintendent at Portsmouth to provide a figurehead design and estimate for approval. The Hellyers of Cosham submitted a design, in June 1855, with an estimate of cost of £24.10.0. The approval letters of this date are not held at the National Archives, Kew, but, as Aurora was the Roman Goddess of the Dawn, there would probably have been a reference to the dawn in the figurehead's trailboards.

Commissioned in Plymouth in November 1863 for the Channel Squadron, one of her first duties was to escort the Prince and Princess of Wales (later King Edward VII and Queen Alexandra) to Copenhagen and the Baltic. In 1865 she joined the North America and West Indies Squadron, where she served in the St Lawrence River. Her ship's company manned the gunboats on the Great Lakes of Canada during the period of threat from the Fenian movement.

The engraving of her 'in Winter Quarters at Quebec' shows what an evolution it must have been to prepare ships such as this for the Canadian winter. Lowering of the spars, the topmasts and topgallant masts, and the equivalent parts of her bowsprit, with all the associated standing rigging, must have been a real test of her seamen's skills. Then the ship had to be roofed in to make the interior habitable and all settled in until the thaw, when the whole process had to be reversed.

H.M.S. AURORA IN WINTER QUARTERS AT QUEBEC.—SEE PAGE 398.

HMS *Aurora* – At Quebec in 1867. (Illustrated London News)

In 1874 she became the sea-going training ship for boys and then the guardship at Greenock on the Clyde, before paying off at Plymouth and being broken up in 1881.

Her figurehead was added to the Devonport collection, where she was listed in the 1911 Admiralty Catalogue, and then in the 1914 article on Devonport Figureheads, published in *The Mariner's Mirror* – being amongst those in the Fire Engine House (see page 21).

By 1936 the move to display relics of the Royal Navy's history had driven her outside and the Plymouth Command report recorded that she was situated at the Pier Head of the RN Barracks. During the 1950s, she was one of the figureheads that was coated in fibreglass in the hope that this would give her long-standing protection from the elements – an aspiration that was proved to be wrong.

Work to prepare the figurehead for display at The Box was undertaken by Mainmast Conservation of Little Trethvas, near Helston, Cornwall, including the removal of the resin and fibreglass skin.

HMS *Aurora* – 1936. (Author)

HMS *Topaze*

Built in Devonport Dockyard and launched there in May 1858, HMS *Topaze* was a wooden screw frigate of fifty-one guns. Her figurehead was a three-quarter-length female bust wearing a tiara and a tailored blouse.

As Frederick Dickerson was the resident figurehead carver at Devonport when HMS *Topaze* was being built there, the Admiral Superintendent forwarded a Dickerson design to the Surveyor of the Navy in August 1856 with an estimated cost of £28.10.0. The design and estimate were approved.

This design drawing is not held with the letters of approval at the National Archives, Kew, as it was retained by the carver for use when he was creating the actual figurehead. As already described in the chapter on the figurehead carvers, this design emerged with many others in 2004 as one of the 140 or so drawings in Tasmania in the Dickerson Archive, having been handed down through the family. The shorthand 'Appd.' beside the design shows that it was approved in London by the Surveyor of the Navy.

The 1858 HMS *Topaze* was the third ship of that name to have served in the Royal Navy, the first being a French ship, *La Topaze*, which was handed over as a prize by French royalists at Toulon in 1793. In recognition of the origin of the name, subsequent ships retained the French spelling. Unlike ship names with their origins

Figurehead Design – HMS *Topaze*. (Dickerson)

HMS *Topaze* – 1936. (Author)

in Greek mythology, there was no subject to which the carver could allude, and therefore the trailboards are empty, except for the decorated scroll.

HMS *Topaze* commissioned in 1859 for the Channel Squadron and, for almost twenty years, served twice in the Pacific and then in the Detached Squadron, before becoming the Coastguard Ship at Kingstown, St Vincent, in 1877. She paid off in Plymouth in 1878 before being sold to Castles, shipbreakers, in 1884.

Her figurehead must have been removed in Devonport before the ship was sold. It was photographed in the Fire Engine House in an 1897 article in *The Navy and Army Illustrated* and was later listed in the Devonport collection in the 1911 *Admiralty Catalogue of Pictures, Plate, Relics, &c.*

By 1936 the figurehead had been mounted at the pier-head of the RN Barracks and was later moved indoors to the drill-shed and then the Naval Base Museum. The restoration, repainting and remounting of the figurehead, in preparation for the display at The Box, was undertaken by Orbis Conservation of Greenwich.

HMS *Calcutta*

Built in India at Bombay Dockyard and launched there in March 1831, HMS *Calcutta* was a Third Rate ship of eighty-four guns. Her figurehead was a three-quarter-length bust of an Indian ruler in traditional dress.

HMS *Calcutta* was one of over thirty ships built for the Royal Navy in Bombay during the nineteenth century. She was the fourth eighty-four-gun ship to be built there and, like the other ships that came from that dockyard, was built of teak. She sailed for Portsmouth shortly after her launch.

As might be expected, her figurehead was an elaborately carved Indian ruler, heavily moustached and wearing a beaded turban and a decorated cummerbund into which was tucked a 'Khanjar', a personal weapon of self-defence carried by nobility and royalty. The trailboards carried deeply carved representations of flora, each being symbolic of India – lotus flowers, mangoes and figs of the banyan tree.

The ship commissioned in 1840 and served in the Mediterranean for two years before returning to Plymouth, where she was laid up until 1854. During that period, she was fitted out for active service, an evolution that was assisted by the crew of HMS *Albion* and enthusiastically reported in the *Illustrated London News*.

When war with Russia was declared in 1853, Britain and France agreed to despatch a fleet to the Baltic to protect national interests and to blockade the Russian fleet, preventing them from taking part in the hostilities in the Black Sea. In April 1854, *Calcutta* recommissioned and sailed in the second fleet of ships for the Baltic. She was awarded the battle honour 'Baltic 1855'. Of the figureheads now suspended at The Box, the Indian figure on the bow of HMS *Calcutta* would probably

THE CALCUTTA.

HMS *Calcutta* – Fitting out, 1846. (Illustrated London News)

have patrolled the waters of the Baltic with the mythological man-cum-horse of HMS *Centaur*!

In 1856 HMS *Calcutta* was fitted out for service as the flagship of Admiral Sir Michael Seymour and sailed for China and the Second China War, including the bombardment of Canton in 1856 and the Battle of Fatshan Creek in 1857. She was awarded the battle honour 'China 1856–60' and so, in those waters, the Indian ruler may have caught the eye of the mythical female, Sibyl, who reported the prophecies of the gods, mounted on the bow of HMS *Sybille*!

Returning to Plymouth, HMS *Calcutta* was placed in Ordinary in 1859 until she was towed to Portsmouth in 1863 for experimental gunnery purposes. She returned to Devonport in 1897, where she became one of the two ships that together formed the gunnery school, HMS *Cambridge*.

When the ship was sold to Castles of Plymouth for breaking up, the figurehead was cut from her bow and taken away by horse and cart, not to a museum but to become a farewell gift to the First Sea Lord, Admiral Lord Fisher, who was to retire in 1911. The Admiralty Board knew that, as a midshipman, Lord Fisher had served in HMS *Calcutta* during her 1855 deployment to the Baltic, and so the Indian ruler started what must have been a long and difficult journey to Thetford, in Norfolk, where the admiral was having Kilverstone Hall built for his retirement.

HMS *Calcutta* – 1907. (Hunter)

HMS
Calcutta.
(Hunter)

The bust, complete with its trailboard carvings, was mounted in the grounds and there he stood for over 100 years, at times protected by a shelter, but mostly exposed to the elements.

As he was in private hands, the figurehead was not included in the 1911 *Admiralty Catalogue of Pictures, Plate, Relics &c.*, but he did appear in the 1912 John Player & Sons set of twenty-five cigarette cards, as has already been seen in the introduction to these figurehead chapters.

The Fisher family records show that he was professionally restored in the mid-twentieth century but thereafter was left outside and unprotected. Thus, in 2011, when the figurehead was found to need urgent attention, it was sold to the National Museum of the Royal Navy for reconstruction and remounting. This work was undertaken in the workshop of Rod Hare, creative sculptor and artist of Bickleigh, Devon.

Further restoration, remounting and repainting in preparation for the display at The Box was undertaken by Orbis Conservation of Greenwich.

Preliminary sketch for Hermes. (Dickerson)

HMS *Defiance*

Built in Pembroke Dockyard and launched there in March 1861, HMS *Defiance* was a screw Second Rate ship of eighty-one guns. Her figurehead was the bust of a warrior wearing a plumed helmet and a tunic of scale armour with lion-mask shoulders.

As Pembroke Dockyard did not employ a resident figurehead carver, the Surveyor of the Navy invited the Admiral Superintendent at Portsmouth to provide a figurehead design and estimate for approval. In April 1859 the Hellyers of Portsmouth submitted a design of a helmeted warrior that was appropriate for a ship with such a warlike name and an estimate of £40.0.0.

That design appears never to have been approved as a very similar figurehead had been authorised four years earlier for HMS *Repulse* and had been carved before that ship was renamed HMS *Victor Emanuel*, in honour of the King of Sardinia, making the warrior figurehead inappropriate. The Hellyers were therefore invited to estimate the cost of altering the *Repulse* figurehead to fit HMS *Defiance* and, when the cost estimate was only £4, the work was approved!

HMS *Defiance* did not commission until 1884 and, even then, saw no sea-service, becoming the Torpedo and Mining School of the Plymouth Command.

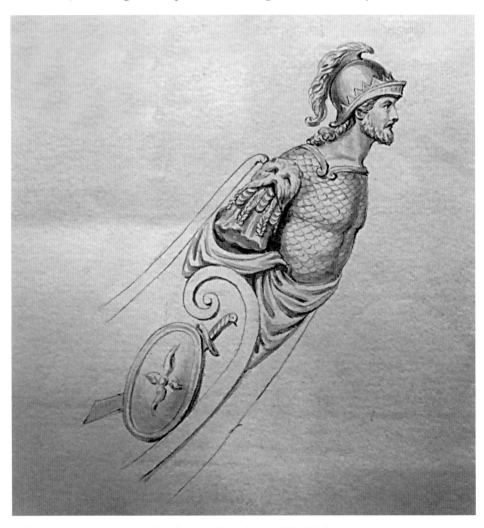

Hellyer Design – HMS *Repulse*, then HMS *Defiance*. (The National Archives)

She was moved to Wilcove, near Torpoint, and was joined by other ships to provide accommodation under the overall name of HMS *Defiance*. Her last days afloat created their own record as, when she was sold to Castle's the shipbreakers in 1931, she was the last of the old wooden walls to fly the White Ensign – afloat and in commission.

The *Defiance* figurehead was preserved on board the ships that had assumed their training role and, when in 1972 the establishment became the Devonport Fleet Maintenance Base, the figurehead was mounted outside their new building in the naval base. Incorporated into the Devonport Heritage Collection, the figurehead was conserved and rebuilt for display at The Box, partly by Hugh Harrison, Consultant and Contractor of West Anstey, Devon, and partly by Orbis Conservation of Greenwich.

HMS *Defiance* –
1936. (Author)

HMS *Tamar*

Built by Samuda Brothers of Poplar and launched there in January 1863, HMS *Tamar* was an iron screw troopship that was barque-rigged; her two foremost masts being square-rigged while her mizzen was fore-and-aft rigged. She had two figureheads, the first being a three-quarter-length male representing the spirit of the River Tamar.

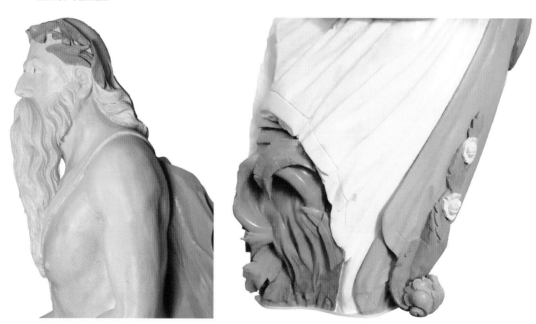

Having been built in a commercial yard, the cost of HMS *Tamar*'s figurehead would have been included in the overall cost of the ship and no separate figurehead design would be expected. However, the three-quarter-length male figure was clearly intended to represent a river spirit appropriate to the River Tamar, with rushes carved in the trailboard area.

Commissioned in 1863, she carried troops initially to the Cape and to China, and, in 1874, was with the naval squadron off the Gold Coast of West Africa, where the King of the Ashanti was opposed to colonial rule by the British and the Dutch. A naval brigade that fought ashore included sailors from HMS *Tamar* and she was awarded the battle honour 'Ashantee 1873–74'. By 1882 she was with the force that bombarded Alexandria, having made three trooping runs from Portsmouth to Malta that year.

It is not clear why or when the figurehead of HMS *Tamar* was changed, but the bearded male figure was landed in Devonport and was replaced with a three-quarter-length female figure with long flowing hair. It cannot have been because of damage or rot as the original carving survived in good shape. Perhaps it was the whim of a new commanding officer but, by 1897, when she relieved HMS *Victor Emanuel* as the receiving ship in Hong Kong, it was the female figure that adorned her bow.

A familiar sight in many historic photographs of Hong Kong harbour, HMS *Tamar*'s end came in December 1941. When invasion of the colony by

HMS *Tamar* – Replacement Figurehead. (Hunter)

HMS *Tamar* – (Author)   The H. M. S. Tamar.   The Harbour receiving Ship.

HMS *Tamar* – 1936. (Author)

Japanese forces was inevitable, she was scuttled to avoid her being used by the invading power.

HMS *Tamar's* original figurehead was amongst those shown to be in the Fire Engine House in an 1897 article in *The Navy and Army Illustrated* and was later listed as being at Devonport Dockyard in the 1911 *Admiralty Catalogue of Pictures, Plate, Relics, &c.*

By 1936 the figurehead was still indoors, but, by the annual survey of 1947, he had been moved to stand beside the road to the main gate, where the accident must have happened to his right arm, which, when 'reset', assumed its new position.

The restoration, repainting and remounting of the figurehead in preparation for the display at The Box was undertaken by Orbis Conservation of Greenwich.

HMS *Windsor Castle* – then HMS *Cambridge*

Built in Pembroke Dockyard and launched there in August 1858, HMS *Windsor Castle w*as a screw three-decker of 100 guns. Her figurehead was a three-quarter-length demi-head of Queen Victoria, crowned and holding the orb and sceptre.

The ship had originally been ordered in 1844 as HMS *Victoria*, a sailing three-decker, but she remained on the stocks for fourteen years, pending decisions on how steam propulsion should be applied to new ships of the Fleet.

As Pembroke Dockyard did not employ a resident figurehead carver, the Surveyor of the Navy instructed the Superintendent at Portsmouth to provide a figurehead design, which Messrs. Hellyer & Sons did in January 1849 with an estimate of £52.0.0. It shows Queen Victoria very much as she may be seen in the figurehead today, except that she has been drawn with the sash of the Order of the Garter over her right – rather than her left – shoulder. The error was obviously spotted and corrected between approval of the design and carving the figurehead itself.

Hellyer Design – HMS *Windsor Castle*. (The National Archives)

Launch of HMS *Windsor Castle*. (Phillips)

Queen Victoria was a most popular subject for the warships of the day, being carved for the bows of the 1839 HMS *Queen*, the 1842 HMS *Superb*, the 1851 HMS *Sans Pareil* and the 1853 HMS *Majestic*. HMS *Victoria* – still on the stocks at Pembroke Dockyard – had her name changed to *Windsor Castle* in January 1855 but kept her royal figurehead – being followed by more in the queen's likeness: the 1857 *Royal Sovereign* and the next 1859 HMS *Victoria*, then building in Portsmouth Dockyard.

While still on the stocks, HMS *Windsor Castle* was converted to steam propulsion. Some of her contemporary ships were 'cut down' – having the upper gun deck removed to allow for the extra weight of machinery etc. Others were lengthened but, in her case, she emerged in August 1858 as a screw three-decker of 100 guns.

Unfortunately, despite the expensive delays, she was found on sea trials to have such poor sea-keeping qualities that she saw no sea service. In 1869 she was renamed HMS *Cambridge* and became the gunnery training school at Devonport. With the rapid development of gunnery in the fleet, gunnery training was urgently needed, and this gave her a useful role for the next twenty-five years. She was joined by HMS *Calcutta* from Portsmouth when the training role there moved ashore.

When gunnery training facilities were built ashore at Devonport, HMS *Cambridge* was sold to Cox of Falmouth for breaking up.

HMS *Cambridge* – 1907. (Hunter)

The figurehead was brought ashore but, despite her royal identity and her sixty years' service, she lost her identity! In the 1913 article in *The Mariner's Mirror*, she was photographed and described as being 'near the barracks', but without a name. By 1931 she was identified as having come from HMS *Royal Adelaide* and this is how she was named in the 1936 Plymouth Command muster.

This incorrect identification followed her to the Royal Naval Engineering College, Manadon, when she was moved there in the early 1970s and it took a visit to the college by the Prince of Wales in 1980 to recognise the error. He immediately saw that the figurehead was in the likeness of Queen Victoria and not Queen Adelaide and hurried research resulted in her being correctly identified again!

When the Engineering College closed in 1995, the figurehead was moved to the gunnery range at Wembury – another HMS *Cambridge* – until its closure in 2001, when it was added to the Devonport Heritage Collection. The figurehead was conserved and rebuilt for The Box by Hugh Harrison, Consultant and Contractor of West Anstey, Devon, who had overseen her earlier restoration in 1986.

HMS *Windsor Castle* – 1936. (Author)

HMS *Royal William*

Built in Pembroke Dockyard, South Wales, and launched there in April 1833, HMS *Royal William* was a First Rate ship of 120 guns. Her figurehead was a full-length standing figure of King William IV.

As there were no figurehead carvers at Pembroke Dock, carved work for warships being built there was created by the carvers at either Portsmouth or Plymouth, that for HMS *Royal William* being carved by the Dickersons of Plymouth. The letters authorising this work are not amongst those at the National Archives but, with her build nearing completion, a letter of November 1832 to Plymouth hastened its delivery.

The king is crowned and wearing the ceremonial robes of the Order of the Garter with no less than three orders of chivalry round his neck. Uppermost is the Scottish Order of the Thistle – identified by the central star and its blue saltire cross – next is the Irish Order of St Patrick – with its central harp – and finally the English Order of the Garter, from which is suspended 'The George' – a miniature of St George slaying the dragon. On the king's left breast, he wears the star of the Order of the Garter.

Measuring more than 13 feet tall, this was a patriotic tribute to the new monarch, who was in the third year of his reign and had served in the Royal Navy as the Duke of Clarence, being known to his subjects as 'The Sailor King'.

HMS *Royal William* spent some years in Ordinary at Plymouth before commissioning in 1854 for service in the Baltic, being one of the fleet that was sent there to blockade the Russian fleet in response to their expansion in the Black Sea. She was awarded the battle honour 'Baltic 1854'. In all probability, of the figureheads now displayed in The Box, the regal figure of King William IV on the bow of HMS *Royal William* would have come face-to-face with the turbaned Egyptian on the bow of HMS *Sphynx*.

One of the lessons learned during the Crimean War was the operational benefit of steam power over sail and, as a result, a lengthy conversion programme followed

HMS *Royal William*. (Phillips)

on many of the ships of the 'sailing navy'. Thus in 1859, HMS *Royal William* was taken in hand at Devonport Dockyard for conversion to steam propulsion. In her case this involved being 'cut down', an operation that involved the removal of the whole of the upper gun-deck and its guns to compensate for the additional weight of the machinery and coal bunkers. As a result, the former 'three-decker' First Rate of 120 guns emerged in February 1860 as a screw 'two-decker' of seventy-two guns.

With her upper gun-deck removed, the standing figure of King William was then too tall to fit under the ship's bowsprit and a replacement, in the form of a bust, was ordered. Frederick Dickerson's design was submitted with an estimate of £35.0.0. but was only approved providing 'the crown is to be made larger and brought down lower on the head'. The design here is amongst those retained in the

Figurehead
Design – HMS
Royal William.
(Dickerson)

Dickerson Archive and shows how the carver planned to implement the Surveyor's instructions.

HMS *Royal William* never commissioned as a steam vessel and in 1884 was transferred to the Liverpool Catholic Reformatory Association, as a training ship for boys, under the name *Clarence*. She was burnt by accident in 1899 in the Mersey and the bust of King William was lost.

Meanwhile, back in Devonport Dockyard, the standing figurehead had been brought ashore and had been placed on a stone plinth beside No. 1 Covered Slip, at the southern tip of the dockyard. Photographs taken of him at this site in the 1890s show him painted white and, not unnaturally, have led to discussions on how he had been painted when afloat. When Douglas Owen wrote about the Devonport Collection in 1914, he assumed that the large examples that were standing outside various buildings had been painted white as 'a dockyard economy measure', but recent paint sampling has proved otherwise.

Affectionally known as 'King Billy', this magnificent figurehead has acted as a beacon to ships based in Devonport for well over a century, wishing them well as they sailed on their operations in both war and peace and welcoming them home on their return.

In all those years the king suffered in several different ways. During the Blitz in 1941, the bombing shook him off his pedestal and he was said to have fallen into the water. In a 1974 restoration he was found to be suffering from 'water on the

HMS *Royal William* – 1897. (The Navy & Army Illustrated)

knee' – rainwater had penetrated his shoulder and had made its way to his left knee! Finally, when the replica was being cast in 2004 so that the original carving could be safely housed indoors, a musket ball was found to be embedded in his right leg! Who fired that shot is yet to be discovered.

During the figurehead's conservation in preparation for display at The Box, paint samples were taken from various parts of the carving and cross sections were examined under a microscope. Up to forty layers of paint were found in some samples with traces of dirt between many of the layers. While the most recent layers were found to be coloured, the older ones were consistently white or cream/off white. At least as far as this figurehead is concerned, further discussion on paint schemes are now unnecessary.

By 1936 when the figureheads were photographed for the *Record of the Figureheads in H M Naval Establishments under Plymouth Command* the figurehead of HMS *Royal William* had been painted in full colour.

The conservation work, paint analysis and repainting of the figurehead in preparation for the display at The Box were undertaken by Orbis Conservation of Greenwich.

HMS *Royal William* – 1936. (Author)

The Devonport Directory

This Directory lists all the figureheads that are known to have been included in the Devonport collection over the years. The dates quoted are the year of the ship's launch and the year in which she was sold, broken up or taken to pieces.

The fourteen figureheads that are on display at The Box are shown in **bold** type to show how this collection compares with the Devonport holdings over the years. The others in the table are listed with either their present location or, if now lost, with a brief explanation of their fate.

Ship	Dates	Ship Type	Figurehead	Location/Fate
Ajax	1809–1864	Third Rate	Warrior bust	To NMM 1936
Amazon	1799–1817	Fifth Rate	Amazon	Lost, Great Fire 1840
America	1810–1827	Third Rate	Female bust	Lost, Great Fire 1840
Arachne	1847–1866	Sloop	Female bust	Lost in Blitz 1941
Atalanta	1847–1868	Brig	Female bust, three-quarter-length	To NMM 1936
Aurora	**1861–1881**	**Screw frigate**	**Female bust**	**The Box**
Basilisk [1]	**1848–1882**	**Paddle sloop**	**Female bust**	**The Box**
Berwick	1809–1821	Third Rate	Male figure	Lost, Great Fire 1840
Black Prince	1861–1904	Armoured frigate	Male, three-quarter-length	Lost without trace [2]
Blenheim	1813–1865	Third Rate	Male bust	To NMM 1936
Cadmus	**1856–1879**	**Screw corvette**	**Male bust**	**The Box**
Calcutta	**1831–1908**	**Second Rate**	**Male bust, three-quarter-length**	**The Box [3]**
Calliope	**1837–1883**	**Sixth Rate**	**Female bust**	**The Box**
Cambridge	1815–1869	Third Rate	A lion & shield	Lost by decay *c.* 1947
Canopus	1798–1887	Third Rate	Male bust	To NMM 1936
Centaur	**1845–1864**	**Paddle frigate**	**A centaur**	**The Box**
Cleopatra	1779–1814	Fifth Rate	Cleopatra	Lost, Great Fire 1840
Clown [4]	1836–1867	Screw gunboat	A jester	To NMM
Conqueror	1801–1822	Third Rate	Male figure	Lost, Great Fire 1840

Constance	1846–1875	Fourth Rate	Female, half-length	Not known
Creole	1845–1875	Sixth Rate	Female bust	Lost in Blitz 1941
Defence	1861–1898	Iron ship	Helmeted head	Not known
Defiance [5]	**1861–1931**	**Screw Second Rate**	**Warrior bust**	**The Box**
Edgar	1779–1835	Third Rate	Male figure	Lost, Great Fire 1840
Encounter	1873–1888	Screw corvette	Male bust	To HMAS *Cerberus* 1952
Favourite	1829–1859	Sloop	Female bust, three-quarter-length	To NMM 1936
Fox	1829–1882	Fifth Rate	Male bust	Lost by decay 1961
Gannet	1857–1877	Screw sloop	A gannet	To NMM 1936
Goliath	1781–1812	Third Rate	Goliath	Lost, Great Fire 1840
Grecian	1838–1865	Brig-sloop	Female bust, three-quarter-length	Lost in Blitz 1941
Harlequin	1836–1860	Brig-sloop	Female bust, three-quarter-length	To NMM 1936
Himalaya [6]	1854–1895	Screw troopship	Male figure, three-quarter-length	To NMM 1936
Hogue	1811–1865	Third Rate	A lion and shield	To NMM 1936
Horatio	1807–1865	Fifth Rate	Bust of Nelson	To NMM 1936
Hussar	1807–1833	Fifth Rate	A hussar	Lost, Great Fire 1840
Indus	1839–1898	Second Rate	Male bust	Lost without trace
Kent	1798–1881	Third Rate	Standing male	Lost in Blitz 1941
Leda	1828–1906	Fifth Rate	Female bust	To NMM 1936
Lion	1847–1905	Second Rate	A lion and shield	Lost without trace
London	1840–1884	Second Rate	Female bust	To NMM 1936
Magicienne	1849–1866	Paddle frigate	Female bust, three-quarter-length	Lost in Blitz 1941
Malta	1800–1840	Second Rate	Knight of Malta	Lost, Great Fire 1840
Megara	1849–1871	Screw frigate	Female bust, three-quarter-length	To NMM 1936
Minerva [7]	**1820**	**Fifth Rate**	**Standing female**	**The Box**
Minx	1846–1859	Screw gunboat	Male bust	Lost without trace [8]
Nelson [9]	1814–18**	First Rate	Bust of Nelson	Lost, Great Fire 1840
Ocean	1761–1793	Second Rate	Bust of Neptune	Lost, Great Fire 1840
Pelorus	1857–1869	Screw corvette	Male bust	Lost in Blitz 1941
Peterel	1860–1885	Screw sloop	Female bust, three-quarter-length	NMRN Portsmouth
Prince of Wales	1860–1869	First Rate	Male bust	Scottish Mar. Mus.
Princess Alice	1844–1878	Paddle packet	Female bust, three-quarter-length	NMRN (Portsmouth)
Raleigh	1873–1905	Screw frigate	Male bust	At HMS *Raleigh*, Torpoint
Rinaldo [10]	1860–884	Screw sloop	Male figure, three-quarter-length	Devonport Heritage Collection
Rattlesnake	1861–1882	Screw corvette	Male bust	Lost in Blitz, 1941
Resistance	1861–1885	Armoured frigate	Male bust	Scottish Mar. Mus.
Royal George	1827–1875	First Rate	Male bust	To NMM 1936
Royal Sovereign	1786–1825	First Rate	George III	Lost, Great Fire 1840
Royal William	**1833–1885**	**First Rate`**	**William IV**	**The Box**
Russell	1822–1865	Third Rate	Male bust	To NMM 1936
St George	1840–1883	First Rate	Standing male	Lost in Blitz 1941

Satellite	1855–1879	Screw corvette	Female bust, three-quarter-length	At HMS *Calliope*
Seagull	1868–1887	Screw gunvessel	A seagull	To NMM 1936
Semiramis	1808–1844	Fifth Rate	Standing female	To NMM 1936
Seringapatam	1819–1873	Fifth Rate	Male on eagle	To NMM 1936
Serpent	1887–1890	Torpedo cruiser	Male, full-length	To NMM 1936
Sphynx	**1846–1881**	**Paddle sloop**	**Male bust**	**The Box**
Squirrel	1853–1879	Brig-sloop	Female demi-figure	Lost without trace [11]
Stag	1830–1866	Fifth Rate	Stag's head	Lost without trace [12]
Stirling Castle	1811–1839	Third Rate	A highlander	Lost, Great Fire 1840
Styx	1841–1866	Paddle sloop	Male bust	Lost in Blitz 1941
Sultan	1775–1805	Third Rate	Grand Turk	Lost, Great Fire 1840
Surprise [13]	1812–1822	Fifth Rate	Female figure, three-quarter-length	Lost in Blitz 1941
Sybille	**1847–1866**	**Fifth Rate**	**Female full-length**	**The Box**
Tamar	**1863–1841**	**Troopship**	**Male full-length**	**The Box**
Terrible	1845–1879	Paddle frigate	Male bust	Lost without trace [14]
Terror	1856–1902	Floating battery	Male bust	Lost at Bermuda
Thalia	1869–1891	Screw corvette	Female bust, three-quarter-length	Lost without trace [15]
Topaze	**1858–1884**	**Screw frigate**	**Female bust, three-quarter-length**	**The Box**
Tribune	1853–1866	Screw corvette	Male bust	To NMM 1936
Union	1811–1833	Second Rate	Male figure	Lost, Great Fire 1840
Wellington [16]	1816–1862	Third Rate	Male bust	Devonport Heritage Collection
Windsor Castle	1790–1839	Second Rate	Edward III	Lost, Great Fire 1840
Windsor Castle	**1858–1869**	**First Rate**	**Queen Victoria, three- quarter-length**	**The Box**

Notes:
1. Basilisk – Not in 1911 Catalogue. Transferred from Flag Officer Sea Training 2001.
2. Black Prince – Not in 1911 Catalogue. First photographed in Devonport collection *c.* 1893.
3. Calcutta – Not in 1911 Catalogue. Bought by NMRN from Lord Fisher in 2012.
4. Clown – Recorded in the 1911 Catalogue as 'Jester'.
5. Defiance – Not in 1911 Catalogue. Transferred from Royal Navy in 2012.
6. Himalaya – Not in 1911 Catalogue. First photographed in Devonport collection 1897.
7. Minerva – Carved for, but never fitted to the 1820 HMS *Minerva*.
8. Minx – Last seen Royal William Yard, Plymouth.
9. Nelson – The original bust and supporters.
10. Rinaldo – Transferred from HMS *Raleigh*, Torpoint, in 2003.
11. Squirrel – Last seen at WRNS quarters, St Budeaux, Plymouth.
12. Stag – Last seen at WRNS quarters, St Budeaux, Plymouth.
13. Surprise – First listed in the Record of Plymouth Command *c.* 1945.
14. Terrible – Last seen Gunnery School Devonport *c.* 1930.
15. Thalia – Last seen Annual Survey, 1947.
16. Wellington – Formerly HMS Hero. Not in 1911 Catalogue.

References &
Further Reading

Original Documents

Dickerson Archive (The) – *Original Drawings* (Now at the National Maritime Museum)
Harrison, H, *Report on the Devonport Collection of Figureheads* (West Anstey, 2012)
Harrison, H, *Report on the Devonport Collection of Figureheads* (West Anstey, 2016)
Navy Board Records – *In-Letters* (The National Archives, ADM 106)
Surveyor of the Navy – *In-Letters Relating to Ships* (The National Archives, ADM 87)

Printed Works

Admiralty, *Catalogue of Pictures, Presentation Plate, Figureheads, Models, Relics and Trophies at The Admiralty, on board H. M. Ships; and in the Naval Establishments at Home and Abroad* (London, 1911)
Anon, *A Record of the Figureheads in HM Naval Establishments under Plymouth Command* (Plymouth, 1936)
Anon, *Figure-Heads*, The Strand Magazine (London, 1891)
Anon, *Figure-Heads of the Royal Navy*, Leisure Hour (London, 1898–99)
Carr Laughton, L. G., *Old Ship Figure-Heads & Sterns* (London, Conway Maritime Press, 1991)
Colledge, J. J., *Ships of the Royal Navy* (London, Greenhill Books, 1987)
Endacott, A., *Devonport Dockyard - The Great Fire of 1840* (Plymouth, Naval Base Museum, 1998)
Lavery, Brian & Simon Stephens, *Ship Models* (London, Zwemmer, 1995)
Lind, Lew, *Fair Winds to Australia* (New South Wales, Reed Books, 1988).
Manning, T. D. & Walker, C. F., *British Warship Names* (London, Putnam, 1959)
Norton, Peter, *Ships' Figureheads* (Newton Abbot, David & Charles, 1976)
Owen, Douglas, *Figureheads*, The Mariner's Mirror (London 1913)
Owen, Douglas, *The Devonport Figureheads*, The Mariner's Mirror (London, 1914)
Peters, Andrew, *Ship Decoration 1630–1780* (Barnsley, Seaforth Publishing, 2013)
Pulvertaft, David, *The Warship Figureheads of Portsmouth* (Stroud, The History Press, 2009)
Pulvertaft, David, *Figureheads of the Royal Navy* (Barnsley, Seaforth Publishing, 2011)
Pulvertaft, David, *The Colour Schemes of British Warship Figureheads 1727–1900*, The Mariner's Mirror (London, May 2018)
Stopford, T. P., *Admiralty Ships Badges 1919–1994* (Rochester, Stone Frigate, 1996)
Thomas, P. N., *British Figurehead & Ship Carvers* (Wolverhampton, 1995)
Warlow, Lt Cdr B., *Battle Honours of the Royal Navy* (Liskeard, Maritime Books, 2004)
Warlow, Lt Cdr B., *Shore Establishments of the Royal Navy* (Liskeard, Maritime Books, 1992)
Whitfield, H. F., *Plymouth and Devonport in Times of War and Peace* (Plymouth, Chapple, 1900)
Winfield, Rif, *British Warships in the Age of Sail 1817–1863* (Barnsley, Seaforth Publishing, 2014)

Image Acknowledgements

The author and publisher would like to thank the following people/organisations for permission to use copyright material in this book: The Box, Plymouth, for the photographs used on the opening pages of the 'figurehead' chapters, taken under contract by Dom Moore and Wayne Perry (photographers). Also, for the image of the 1840 fire in the dockyard on page 20; the National Archives for permission to use figurehead designs from the Admiralty records on pages 30, 34, 54, 74 and 82; Orbis Conservation for the second detailed shot of the *Tamar* figurehead on page 76; Tim Stopford of Stone Frigate for the Ships Badges on pages 35, 39 and 43; Richard Blundell of Hobart, Tasmania, for the many figurehead designs from the Dickerson Archive, each marked 'Dickerson'; Richard Hunter, of Aughton, near Sheffield, for images from the Hunter Archives on pages 21, 69, 70, 78 and 84; and Lt Cdr Lawrence Phillips of Northwood for images from the Phillips Collection on pages 83 and 88.